How To Show What You Mean During A Presentation

How to use visual techniques to transform a speech into a memorable event

"Practical, proven techniques that will help you to make your next speech a success"

Dr. Jim Anderson

Published by:
Blue Elephant Consulting
Tampa, Florida

Copyright © 2013 by Dr. Jim Anderson

All rights reserved. No part of this book may be reproduced of transmitted in any form or by any means, electronic or mechanical, including photocopying, recording or by any information storage and retrieval system without written permission of the publisher, except for inclusion of brief quotations in a review.

Printed in the United States of America

Library of Congress Control Number: 2013923025

ISBN-13: 978-1494498733
ISBN-10: 1494498731

Warning – Disclaimer

The purpose of this book is to educate and entertain. This book does not promise or guarantee that anyone following the ideas, tips, suggestions, techniques or strategies will be hired. It is the discretion of employers if you will or will not be hired. The author, publisher and distributor(s) shall have neither liability nor responsibility to anyone with respect to any loss or damage caused, or alleged to be caused, directly or indirectly by the information contained in this book.

Recent Books By The Author

Product Management

- Product Management Secrets: Techniques For Product Managers To Boost Product Sales And Increase Customer Satisfaction

- Customer Lessons For Product Managers: Techniques For Product Managers To Better Understand What Their Customers Really Want

Public Speaking

- How To Rehearse In Order To Give The Perfect Speech: How to effectively rehearse your next speech to that your message be remembered forever!

- Secrets To Creating The Perfect Speech: How to create a speech that will make your message be remembered forever!

CIO Skills

- How CIOs Can Make Innovation Happen: Tips And Techniques For CIOs To Use In Order To Make Innovation Happen In Their IT Department

- CIO Communication Skills Secrets: Tips And Techniques For CIOs To Use In Order To Become Better Communicators

IT Manager Skills

- Secrets Of Effective Leadership For IT Managers: Tips And Techniques That IT Managers Can Use In Order To Develop Leadership Skills

- IT Manager Career Secrets: Tips And Techniques That IT Managers Can Use In Order To Have A Successful Career

Negotiating

- Learn The Skill Of Exploring In A Negotiation: How To Develop The Skill Of Exploring What Is Possible In A Negotiation In Order To Reach The Best Possible Deal

- Learn How To Argue In Your Next Negotiation: How To Develop The Skill Of Effective Arguing In A Negotiation In Order To Get The Best Possible Outcome

Miscellaneous

- Power Distribution Unit (PDU) Secrets: What Everyone Who Works In A Data Center Needs To Know!

- Making The Jump: How To Land Your Dream Job When You Get Out Of College!

Note: See a complete list of books by Dr. Jim Anderson at the back of this book.

Acknowledgements

Any book like this one is the result of years of real-world work experience. In my over 25 years of working for 7 different firms, I have met countless fantastic people and I've been mentored by some truly exceptional ones. Although I've probably forgotten some of the people who made me the person that I am today, here is my attempt to finally give them the recognition that they so truly deserve:

- Thomas P. Anderson
- Art Puett
- Bobbi Marshall
- Bob Boggs

Dr. Jim Anderson

This book is dedicated to my wife Lori. None of this would have been possible without her love and support.

Thanks for the best 21 years of my life (so far)...!

Speaking. Negotiating. Managing. Marketing.

Table Of Contents

DON'T JUST SAY IT, SHOW IT!..8

ABOUT THE AUTHOR..10

CHAPTER 1: TOOLS TO HELP VISUALIZE YOUR NEXT PRESENTATION 15

CHAPTER 2: TOUGH TASKS: HOW TO PRESENT TO CHILDREN 19

CHAPTER 3: ACT UP OR SIT DOWN! 23

CHAPTER 4: MASTERING THE POWERPOINT BEAST IN 3 EASY STEPS 28

CHAPTER 5: ADVANCED POWERPOINT: 3 TIPS THE PROS USE..........32

CHAPTER 6: HOW TO USE POWERPOINT TO KILL YOUR AUDIENCE (FIGURATIVELY)..36

CHAPTER 7: STOP! PUBLIC SPEAKERS NEED TO STEP AWAY FROM POWERPOINT... 40

CHAPTER 8: SPEAKERS LEARN TO MAKE TASTY SPEECHES BY ADDING JUST THE RIGHT SPICES 44

CHAPTER 9: PUBLIC SPEAKERS KNOW THAT THEY HAVE TO COLOR THEIR PRESENTATIONS..48

CHAPTER 10: CREATE POWERPOINT SLIDES, GO TO JAIL 52

CHAPTER 11: 6 TIPS FOR MAKING POWERPOINT WORK WITH YOUR NEXT SPEECH, NOT AGAINST IT 56

CHAPTER 12: HOW TO USE POWERPOINT TO CREATE INTRIGUE IN YOUR NEXT PRESENTATION 60

Don't Just Say It, Show It!

All too often public speakers think that all that they have to work with are the words that will tumble out of their mouth during their next presentation. Whereas these words are important, a speech offers you many other ways to connect with your audience by demonstrating what you are talking about.

The arrival of the PowerPoint and Keynote software programs suddenly made creating slides simple and easy to do. The result of this is that almost all speeches these days seem to include some form of slides. That being said, all too often the slides are not well made and actually end up taking away from the presentation instead of contributing to it.

However, giving a speech that will be able to rise above just the words that you say involves a lot more than just creating and using the right set of slides. It turns out that every speech is actually a performance. What this means for us as speakers is that we need to take some cues from actors and start to deliver more than just a speech – we owe our audience a show.

The words that you use in your speech carry a power all of their own. Yes, you can choose just any old words and you'll be able to get your point across to your audience. However, will they remember what you said? Probably not.

If instead you spend the time researching and picking just the right words then that will make all the difference in the world. Combining powerful words with impressive visuals can transform a run of the mill speech into an event that your audience will be talking about long after you have stopped speaking.

This book has been created to provide you with insights into how you can add different ways to demonstrate what you are talking about to your next speech. We'll discuss the right way to create PowerPoint slides, how to put on a performance for your audience, what it's going to take to add some color to your next speech.

For more information on what it takes to be a great public speaker, check out my blog, The Accidental Communicator, at:

www.TheAccidentalCommunicator.com

Good luck!

- Dr. Jim Anderson

About The Author

I must confess that I never set out to be a public speaker. When I went to school, I studied Computer Science and thought that I'd get a nice job programming and that would be that. Well, at least part of that plan worked out!

My first job was working for Boeing on their F/A-18 fighter jet program. I spent my days programming fighter jet software in assembly language and I loved it. The U.S. government decided to save some money and went looking for other countries to sell this plane to. This put me into an unfamiliar role: I started to meet with foreign military officials and I ended up having to give speeches in order to explain what my product did.

Time moved on and so did I. I found myself working for Siemens, the big German telecommunications company. They were making phone switches and selling them to the seven U.S. phone companies. The problem was that the switches were too complicated. Customers couldn't tell the difference between one complicated phone switch from another complicated phone switch. Once again I found myself standing in front of the room giving speeches in order to explain what these complicated machines did and why ours were better than anyone else's.

I've spent over 25 years working as a product manager for both big companies and startups. This has given me an opportunity to do many, many presentations for customers, at conferences, and everywhere in-between.

I now live in Tampa Florida where I spend my time managing my consulting business, Blue Elephant Consulting, teaching college courses at the University of South Florida, and traveling to work with companies like yours to share the knowledge that I have about how to create and deliver powerful and effective speeches.

I'm always available to answer questions and I can be reached at:

Dr. Jim Anderson
Blue Elephant Consulting
Email: jim@BlueElephantConsulting.com
Facebook: http://goo.gl/1TVoK
Web: **www.BlueElephantConsulting.com**

"Unforgettable communication skills that will set your ideas free..."

Create Speeches That Motivate Your Audiences And Get Your Message Heard!

Dr. Jim Anderson is available to provide training and coaching on the topics that are the most important to people who have to speak in public: how can I create a speech that people want to hear and how can I deliver in a way that will allow me to connect with my audience and get my point across to them?

Dr. Anderson believes that in order to both learn and remember what he says, speakers need to laugh. Each one of his speeches is full of fun and humor so that what he says "sticks" with everyone.

Dr. Anderson's Public Speaking Training Includes:

1. How to plan your next speech: pick your purpose and understand your audience.
2. What's the best way to get PowerPoint and Keynote to work with you, not against you?
3. What do you need to do when you are presenting in order to truly connect with your audience?

Dr. Jim Anderson presents over 100 speeches per year. To invite Dr. Anderson to speak at your event, contact him at:

Phone: 813-418-6970 or
Email: jim@BlueElephantConsulting.com

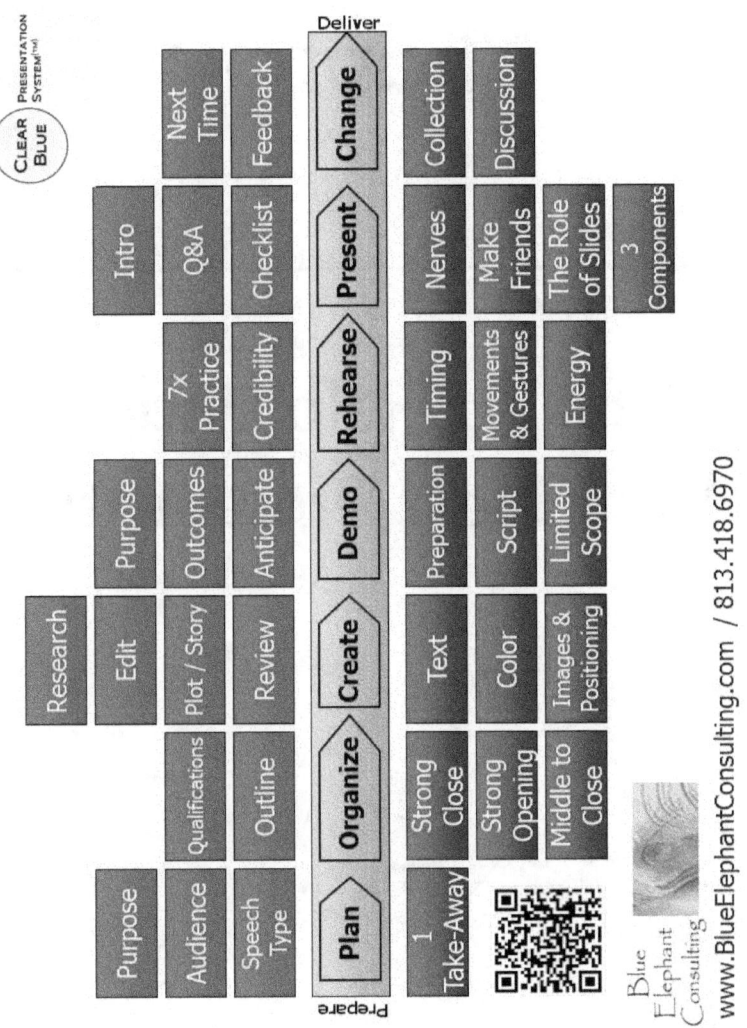

Blue Elephant Consulting has created the **Clear Blue™ Presentation System** for creating and delivering powerful and memorable presentations. The contents of this book are based on lessons learned during the development of the Clear Blue system. Contact Blue Elephant Consulting to learn more about the Clear Blue presentation system.

Chapter 1

Tools To Help Visualize Your Next Presentation

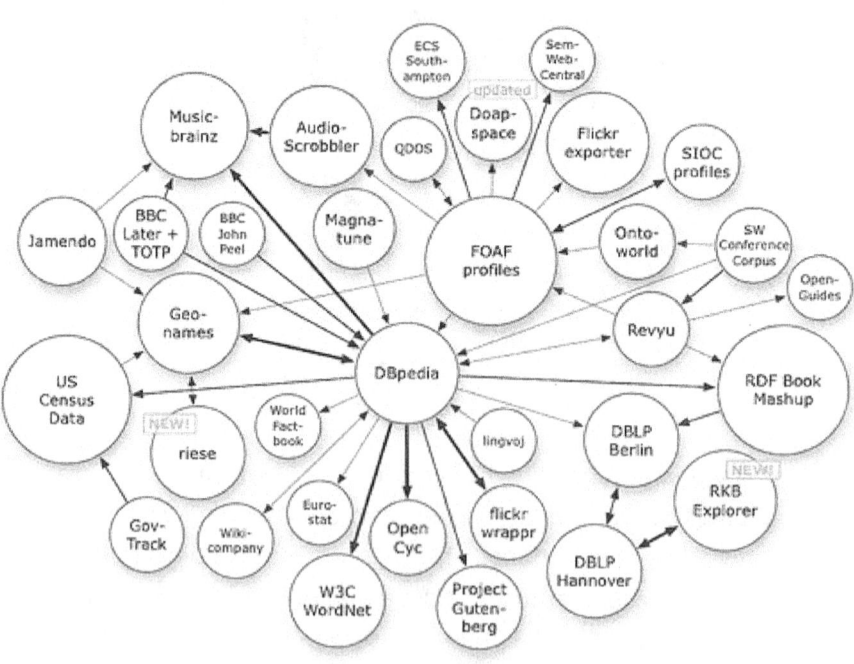

Chapter 1: Tools To Help Visualize Your Next Presentation

We would all like our next presentation to be our best. However, when we've got lots and lots of data to present, we can all too easily overwhelm our audience. What's a presenter to do? It turns out that the good folks over at IBM have come up with a way to help us out of this mess that we've gotten ourselves into...

Not having enough data to support our position is rarely the issue. Rather, having too much data and not enough knowledge that has been created by processing that data IS the issue. Researchers at IBM have set up an experimental web site at **www.many-eyes.com** where you can upload data and then play around with it in order to visualize it.

Now I'm sure that everyone is well aware of the graphing capabilities of both PowerPoint and Excel. The problem is that EVERYONE is aware of these and so all too often, every presentation starts to look the same.

The scientists at IBM's Watson Research Center (located up in Cambridge, Mass.) have created this site not so much to help presenters, but rather to help people publish and discuss graphics in a group. However, there is no reason that we can't make use of the tools that they are providing us with and if we can get some social networking suggestions along the way, all the better.

The web site is the creation of two IBM researchers, Martin Wattenberg and Fernanda Viegas. What they wanted to do was to take the sophisticated data visualization tools that have been available to researchers and make them available to the masses.

Currently, the Many Eyes site provides 16 different ways to present your data. Yes, your old friends the stack graphs and bar charts are there. However there are also more interesting presentations such as diagrams that let people map relationships and TreeMaps which show information in colored rectangles.

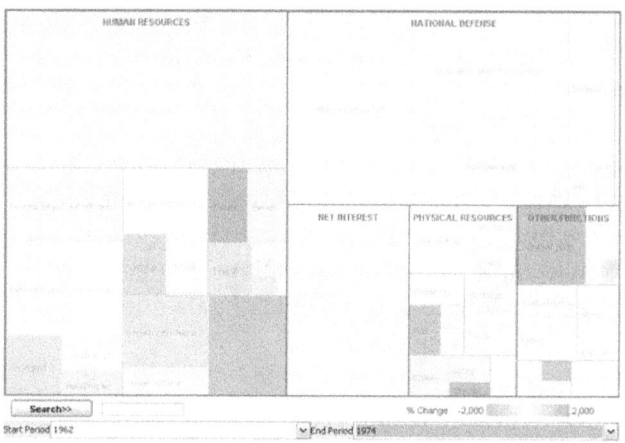

This Is An Example Of A TreeMap Visualization

When the site first became available, they only offered visualization tools that would work with numbers. Quickly the site owners discovered that their users were attempting to upload books and blog posts. Based on this discovery, they went ahead and added visualization techniques that would work with unstructured text.

One of my favorite unstructured tools is the Tag cloud that you've probably been seeing show up on blogs (like mine). The more a word is used, the larger it appears in a tag cloud. Here's an example:

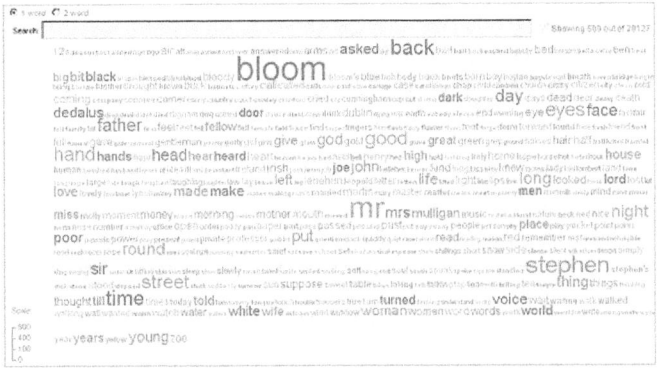

Example of a Tag Cloud Visualization

If you want to learn how to use this tool to process your data, Rich Hoeg has created the **Northstar Nerd Tutorial: Data Visualization via IBM's Many Eyes**.

One important point to realize, the tool was really designed to allow people to share data and visualizations. Don't upload confidential info! You can delete your information after you are done processing it; however, if it has been commented on by others this won't make the site's owners very happy.

Have fun coming up with different ways to look at your data and present it to your audience. However, keep in mind that once you start to look at the data in a different way, it may end up giving you answers to questions that you didn't even know that you had.

Chapter 2

Tough Tasks: How To Present To Children

Chapter 2: Tough Tasks: How To Present To Children

Getting up in front of an audience to give a speech can be a nerve racking experience. If most of the members of that audience are under the age of 10, it can be downright terrifying.

There's no reason to fear the younger set, you just need to adjust both your speech and how you give it in order to be successful. I'm going to tell you how to do both…

It's All About What They See

When we talk to an adult audience, we focus first on what we want to say and then if we have time, we'll think about how we want to say it. When we're addressing an audience that is made up of kids, this thinking needs to be flipped.

Kids at a young age are primarily visual creatures. If you stand in one place and talk at them, they'll never pay attention. Talking without doing anything else for more than a couple of minutes will result in your losing the attention of your young audience.

Instead, you're going to need to use visuals as a part of your speech. We're not talking about just bringing along one thing to hold up at some point during your speech.

Rather, you are going to have to have to bring along a whole group of visuals. This also means that while you are rehearsing your speech, you are going to have to plan out what visuals you'll be using and when you'll use them.

In This Case, Speed Does Not Kill

As presenters, we try to make sure that we don't overwhelm our audiences. One way that we do this is to present our information at a measured, moderate pace that we're sure that they can all keep up with.

However, when you are presenting to a young audience, this is going to be the kiss of death. For kids, slow means boring and boring means that I'm going to be spending my time thinking about other things, not what you are saying.

As speakers, we need to pick up the pace when we are talking to kids. Nothing that we talk about can last for very long. When you are telling a story, you need to quickly get to the point and move on. Kids are not going to sit around waiting for you to build up to your big payoff.

A subtle but very important point is that all of this pick up the pace talk does not mean that you need to talk faster. As adults we talk at about 150 words per minute.

However, studies have shown that our young audiences can only process about 124 words per minute. If you speak too quickly, your audience is not going to be able to understand what you are saying and they'll drift off.

What All Of This Means For You

The good news is that it is possible to give a speech to kids and emerge with your life. However, you can't give the same type of speech that you would give to an adult audience if you want to be successful.

An audience made up of little kids is fundamentally different from an adult audience. This means that you need to change not only what you say, but also how you say it. Kids tune in and pay more attention if you can make your speech more visual – use props and move around more. They will never permit you to deliver a slow speech – you need to keep things moving quickly.

Although speaking to a young audience may seem like a risky thing to do (so much can go wrong), it's well worth the effort. Speakers who can develop the skills to do this well are able to improve their overall speaking ability and this will show every time they give a speech...

Chapter 3

Act Up Or Sit Down!

Chapter 3: Act Up Or Sit Down!

When I come to hear you speak, no matter if it's a departmental project status report or at a local restaurant or even if it was at a convention, the worst thing that you can do is to **waste my time**. What are you going to do about this?

Why So Many Speakers Suck

Let's be frank here – most speakers that you listen to **really aren't that good**. In fact, the ones that we think are good may not really be all that good – they may just be better than the ones who are really bad! What's going on here? It's actually pretty simple, most speakers are boring. Who wants to listen to that?

All too often a speaker will focus exclusively on what they are going to be saying and spend little or no time thinking about **how they are going to say it**.

If you need an analogy to clear things up, this would be like a chef who worries about what ingredients go into a meal without spending any time thinking about how to actually cook the thing. Sure he'll be able to make something, but **it's not going to taste very good**.

Fixing The Problem Of Your Boring Speeches

You are in a rut. You've found a particular speaking style that you believe suits you (that means that it worked once and you've stuck with it ever since) and you have become what we all fear the most – **a boring speaker**. How are we going to fix this problem?

You are going to have to **take action**. You are going to have to start to experiment with the unknown. You are going to have to step into the world of theater.

Birgit Starmanns has spent time in both the world of speaking as well as the world of theater. She points out that actors spend their time working hard to allow the audience **to feel what the actor is currently feeling**. In order to make this happen they use six tools:

- **Quotes**: quotes are a powerful way to invite someone else into your speech. All too often speakers just stick any old quote into their speech in order to give themselves credibility – don't do that. Instead, make sure any person that you invite into your speech by using their quote helps to move your speech along and gives you more creditability with your audience.

- **Roles**: It's just you up there and that can get pretty boring for your audience. How about if you stop being you for a bit and turn into someone else? You need to make it very clear to your audience that you are doing this, otherwise they are going to think that you've all of a sudden lost it. I've used this during internal status reports in order to bring the voice of other departments (e.g. finance) into my presentation.

- **Props**: This is one of the simplest things to use, and yet all too few speakers take the time to think about what props would help them get their point across. In the past during presentations to sales teams, I've used marketing brochures from their competitors that they instantly recognized in order to drive a point home.

- **Staging**: I hate it when a presenter acts like a block of stone and stands in one place during an entire presentation. You've got the entire stage / front of the room / etc. – use it! In fact, as you move from section to section in your speech, move to a different spot to speak and your audience will understand that you've moved on in the speech.

- **Costumes**: Ok, so you've got to be careful here depending on your audience, but you should at least consider it for every speech that you give. I'm not talking about a full on Hollywood costume, but rather wearing something that will enhance your message. I've used a chef's hat during a presentation to show that we were "cooking up" some new products to sell – you get the point.

- **Audience Participation**: Do you feel lucky? Well, do you? Bringing someone from your audience up on stage during a presentation is a huge risk. However, it's a great way to capture everyone's attention – they will all be breathing a sigh of relief that it wasn't them that got picked. If you are ready to interact well with you victim, I mean volunteer, then your speech definitely won't be boring.

Final Thoughts

Anyone can give a boring speech – don't let it be you. You've got to realize that no matter the setting in which you'll be presenting in, be it a boardroom or a convention hall, you are **ultimately putting on a performance** for your audience.

Not everybody is a born entertainer, but that's ok. Where you'll really tick me off is **if you don't at least try**. Theater actors have to connect with their audience every time they put on a show. In order to do this they pull out all of the stops and use every device that they have available to them in order to make their performance unforgettable.

You need to learn from them, research their techniques, and then **apply them** to your next speech where appropriate. You may not turn into the next Robert De Niro or Glenn Close, but that doesn't matter. You won't be giving boring speeches anymore and that's all that matters…!

Chapter 4

Mastering The PowerPoint Beast In 3 Easy Steps

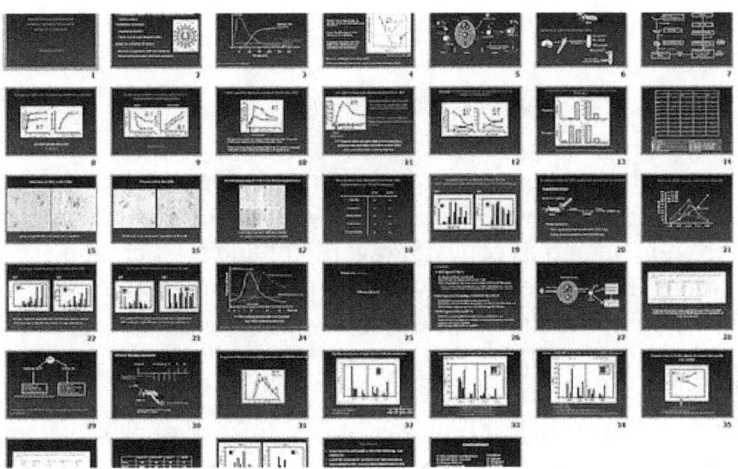

Chapter 4: Mastering The PowerPoint Beast In 3 Easy Steps

Can we all be honest here? PowerPoint is a part of everyone's life no matter how you feel about it. We all seem to fall into **one of three camps**: we fear it, we love it too much, or we just don't really know what to do with it. With a little help, I think that I can help you out here…

Get Your Head Straight

The first thing to work out isn't what your slides need to look like, rather it's **what role PowerPoint should play in your next speech**. The answer is, always, a supporting role.

This means that you need to make sure that your audience doesn't end up spending your entire speech **looking at your slides and not you**. Likewise, you don't want your slides to confuse your audience – almost as if they are telling a different story than what you are talking about.

Speech First, Slides Second – Or Third

If you only remember one thing from reading this, I'm hoping that this is it: always, **always write your speech first**. Don't you dare pop open that copy of PowerPoint and start creating slides until AFTER you've gotten your words all worked out.
Remember: the slides are there to support your speech, not the other way around.

I fully understand just how easy it is to instead of picking up a pen (or a keyboard) and spending some time doing the hard job of writing (unfun) that you open PowerPoint and spend a lot of time drawing (fun!) The problem with this is that you'll end up **creating a lousy speech**.

When your words have to follow your slides, **the slides will take center stage** and you'll be shoved off into a corner. There won't be a natural flow to your words. Instead it will appear as though you are just reading off of each slide as it is displayed. This is no way to give a speech.

Slides Are Like Diamonds – They Should Be Rare

Sadly I suspect that at one time or another we've all had to sit though one of those speeches where the presenter showed up with like **300 slides** and come hell or high water, they were going to show each and every one of them to us.

After you've created your speech and when you start to design some slides, you need to make sure that **you don't turn into that person** with 300 slides. A good way to prevent it is to take a step back and look at your speech.

What is the main point that you are trying to make? You should probably have a slide for that. What are the three ways that you support the main point that you are trying to make? You should probably have slides for those. If you can stop here, that would be a good thing.

Cut Down On The Slides That You Have

The last thing that you're going to want to do is to **throw away some of your slides**. "What?" you say. You heard me, you've got too many slides. I don't care which ones you throw away, just get rid of some of them – they can't all be critical to the message that you are trying to make.

This may be difficult for you to do, **but do it anyway**. Your audience will benefit from it and they'll thank you in the end.

What All Of This Means For You

Repeat after me **"PowerPoint is my friend"**. It can be an important tool that can make your next speech even more powerful; however, you have to know how to use it.

The key things to keep in mind **are simple, but critical**. You must remember to write your speech before you start to create slide. You have to keep the number of slides that you make to a minimum. Finally, you need to make a second pass and throw away as many slides as you possibly can.

Adding multimedia to your next presentation **can only make it better**. Just remember, you are the star of the show, not your slides!

Chapter 5

Advanced PowerPoint: 3 Tips The Pros Use

Chapter 5: Advanced PowerPoint: 3 Tips The Pros Use

PowerPoint is **a double edged sword** when it comes to giving a speech: it can be both a powerful way to add a multimedia impact to your speech or it can end up distracting your audience and taking their attention away from what you have to say. The experts know how to use this tool correctly and here are three of the ways that they tame the PowerPoint beast...

It's All About Look & Feel

The PowerPoint slides that a speaker uses to augment their speech should **look professional**. Now this doesn't mean that they needed to be done by an expensive design house, just that they shouldn't look like they were put together by an amateur (even if they were!)

The most important part of this is to make sure that the slides have **a consistent look and feel** to them. The first step in making this happen is to decide on a PowerPoint template and then use it for your entire presentation.

However, that's not quite enough. All too often I see presenters who've had a presentation that **has been force-fit into a new template**. That it doesn't fit is pretty clear because the text and images spill over the edges and on top of the template's decorations.

As a presenter it's your responsibility to make sure that this doesn't happen to you. Review your slides and make sure that **they are living in harmony** with the template that you are using for this presentation.

Getting From Here To There

PowerPoint is a powerful tool. It has a lot of features that **either enhance your presentation or take away from it** depending on how you use them. One such feature is the "slide transitions".

When you move from one slide to the next, PowerPoint can do a number of amazing things on the screen. **These are what is called a transition.** Transitions can range from the simple (old slide fades away only to be replaced by the new slide) to the complex (new slide zooms out from the center of the screen).

My advice to you here is to **keep it simple**. Just as your PowerPoint slides should not overwhelm your speech so too should your transitions not overwhelm your slides. If your audience is eagerly waiting to see your next transition, then you've done something wrong.

PowerPoint will let you use a different type of transition for each slide. **Don't do this.** Instead pick one type of transition and stick with it for the entire presentation.

No Surprises

Technology is a wonderful thing – until it turns on you! The professional speakers know that although the PowerPoint presentation that they put together while sitting at their desk looked one way, **it might not look that way** when they are standing in front of an audience.

There are a lot of reasons for this: you might be using a different computer, the display system might change one color into another color, etc. The way to overcome such surprises is **to be prepared**.

When you are going to use PowerPoint slides as a part of a presentation, **always try to show up early** in order to run through your slides on the system that will be used to display them and in the space where you'll be giving your speech.

The reason that you want to do this is that you'll be able to **see what your audience will eventually be seeing**. Issues with a slide being too dark, the colors being messed up, or some other technical snafu can be quickly identified and corrected on the spot.

What All Of This Means For You

As speakers, we all need to make use of whatever tools we have available. **PowerPoint is one such tool**. However, if not used correctly, PowerPoint can actually end up diminishing the impact of our speech.

We can avoid the pitfalls and make the most of PowerPoint if we **follow some simple rules**. Making sure that all of the slides in our presentation have a common look and feel is important. Picking a slide transition that doesn't distract from our slides and then using it consistently will boost our impact. Finally, taking the time to preview how our slides are going to look before a presentation can prevent any technical glitches from showing up.

Technology is here to stay and **speakers need to learn how to harness it**. By using PowerPoint the way that the pros do, you can create and deliver powerful multimedia presentations that will leave your audience saying to themselves "That looked professionally done..."

Chapter 6

How To Use PowerPoint To Kill Your Audience (Figuratively)

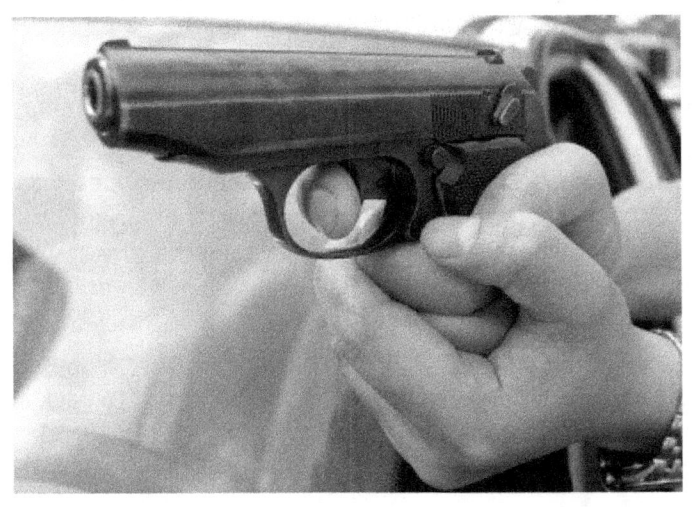

Chapter 6: How To Use PowerPoint To Kill Your Audience (Figuratively)

Hopefully we can all agree that as a speaker, you should never start a speech with intention of killing some or all of your audience– your chances of being asked back go way done if you do. Given this, why are you still using such bad PowerPoint slides?

Shooting Bullets At Your Audience

First things first, how many things can you do at the same time? No, I mean really well? As human beings, we simply don't do a good job of multitasking no matter how well we think that we can do it.

It turns out that when you slap that PowerPoint slide up there with all of those bullets on it, you are asking your audience to make a decision. You are asking them to either pay attention to you or spend their precious attention reading the words on your slide. There's really no way that you can win this game.

Titles Count

So what's a presenter to do? I mean if you create slides, you're going to have to put at least some words on there, right? It turns out that what you need to do is to take the time to make every word count.

This means that, among other things, the title of your slide is now million dollar waterfront property. You've got to pack a clear message into each title: "Status Update" is out, "Update on dramatic drop in 4th quarter profits" is in.

Build Your Own Background

The look and feel of each slide can be determined by not the words that you use, but rather by the background that you choose. Don't make the same mistake that everyone else does.

PowerPoint comes with a set of standard slide backgrounds (lots of blue in them for some reason). The problem with this is that since PowerPoint is so popular and has been around for so long, we've all seen all of them before. The last thing that you want to do is set your audience up to be bored starting with your first slide.

Instead, build your own backgrounds. Instead of choosing a PowerPoint provided background, instead start with a blank background and add pictures, images, and graphics to build up a unique background for each of your slides. This simple but effective technique will give your slides a powerful fresh look.

More IS Better

So how should you handle the case where you do have a lot to say on a given slide? All too often we just bite the bullet (sorry for the pun) and pack all of the words that we want to say into a single slide and hope for the best.

A much better way of doing this is to break a single word-heavy slide up into multiple slides with few words on them. In the past when we were dealing with physical slides we were hesitant to do this because it would have caused a lot of physical effort to switch slides all the time. With today's electronic slides, this is no longer an issue.

What All Of This Means For You

A reality of the world that we speak in is that PowerPoint is here to stay. This means that you're going to have to figure out how to make this beast work with you, not against you.

You don't need to be a professional graphics artist to create a PowerPoint presentation that will enhance your speech. Minimizing the number of words that you use and creating custom slide backgrounds are simple and yet powerful techniques that you can use to be effective.

The great communicators of the past never had PowerPoint slides that they could use. Done correctly, just imagine how much more powerful you'll be with good slides!

Chapter 7

Stop! Public Speakers Need To Step Away From The PowerPoint...

Chapter 7: Stop! Public Speakers Need To Step Away From PowerPoint...

When somebody asks you to give a speech do you start thinking about the PowerPoint (or Keynote for you Mac users) slides that you'll have to create? Do you ask the person **how long the speech needs to be** just in order to determine how many slides that you'll need to make? Stop!

Maybe it's time that we all take a step back from the keyboard and those books about PowerPoint presentation tips and instead spend a moment thinking about when it's appropriate to use PowerPoint – and when it's not!

When Should You Use PowerPoint?

We all like to make fun of PowerPoint – have you heard the phrase "death by PowerPoint"? Even though we dread going to presentations in which other people are going to be showing us their PowerPoint slides, we have no problem **creating volumes of slides** to use in our own presentation.

This all leads to the interesting question: maybe we should all **stop using PowerPoint** all together? Well, maybe — but probably not. PowerPoint has caught on for a reason – it's very good at doing what it was intended to do.

What PowerPoint does well is to help a speaker to boost the importance of their public speaking by helping them to **visually display information**. Things that could require a long explanation in order to make our audience understand what we are talking about can be quickly communicated using PowerPoint.

It gives us the ability to share graphs, charts, photos, and even videos as a part of a speech. This is powerful stuff.

When Should You Not Use PowerPoint?

With all that being said, you might be led to believe that every speech **needs to have a bit of PowerPoint added to it**. Now there you'd be wrong.

Many of the speeches that we give, such as motivational speeches, are really all about the speaker – you. These kinds of speeches call for your audience to use their listening skills, not their eyes in order to learn.

Adding PowerPoint, or even worse the wrong kind of PowerPoint, to this type of speech can take away from your main message.

What's going on here is that we all need to learn how to take a step back and **make a decision about using PowerPoint** with a speech long before we sit down at a keyboard and start to pull our next slide deck together.

The first thing that should come into your mind is the simple fact that you need to decide on **what the purpose of your next speech is**. What is the strategy that you're going to use to get your message across to your audience? Once you know this, then you can consider if PowerPoint will help or hinder your ability to accomplish it.

If you do choose to use PowerPoint then you've got another decision to make. You've got to determine **how many slides** you want to use.

You may be surprised to learn that the correct answer is "as few as possible". You want to use just enough slides to help you get your point across and not one more. Create a slide deck and then go through it cutting out as many slides as you possibly can. When you can cut no more, then you've got the right number of slides.

What All Of This Means For You

PowerPoint is **a powerful tool** that public speakers can use to communicate information . However, if we're not careful we'll end up using it when we really shouldn't.

If you are going to be giving a speech in which your goal is to **communicate information** then using PowerPoint may be a good idea. As always, you need to take steps to make sure that your slides don't overwhelm the message that you are trying to convey.

If instead of communicating information, you are trying to **inspire or motivate an audience**, then think twice about using PowerPoint. Create the strategy that you want to use with your speech and identify the message that you want to get across. Then determine how many, if any, slides you'll need in order to accomplish this task.

As with all powerful tools, PowerPoint can either **help or hinder** your next speech. When asked to speak, spend your time thinking about what you want to accomplish and then determine if PowerPoint can help you do this. Not the other way around!

Chapter 8

Speakers Learn To Make Tasty Speeches By Adding Just The Right Spices

Chapter 8: Speakers Learn To Make Tasty Speeches By Adding Just The Right Spices

What will your audience remember longer: your next speech or a great meal that they've just had? I hate to admit it, but I'm willing to bet that the meal has a better chance of staying on their mind than our speeches. Why is that? Could it be that the meal did a better job of **using spices to create a lasting memory?**

The Reason That Spices Are So Important

The biggest problem with a boring speech isn't that you are going to end up hurting anyone; rather it's that **you are going to bore your audience**. When you are done speaking, a bored audience is going to get up and leave and they're not going to remember anything that you said.

As a speaker this means that we need to find ways to **make our next speech more memorable**. In order to make this happen, we need to understand how our audiences take in information. The way that they do it is to use all five of their senses to detect what is going on all around them.

As speakers this means that we need to tune our next speech so that it activates all of our audience's senses. The more senses that we can get them to use while we give our speech, then the better the chances that we'll have of **them remembering what we told them** long after we've finished speaking.

Call it what you will, but I like to refer to the techniques that we use to reach our audience's various senses "spices". They are **the little things that we add to our speech** that will remove the bland and add some zing. Now the only question is how to go about adding these spices to our next speech.

4 Secrets To Using Spices In Your Next Speech

Even if you don't consider yourself to be much of a cook, **you can still add spices to your next speech**. The trick is to simply know what kind of spices are available to you in your "speech kitchen".

The first spice that we all can use is the **power of being descriptive**. As you build your speech, take the time to carefully choose your words. Use words that your audience already knows and has powerful associations with to bring your audience into your speech.

Next, **add a dash of the dynamic**. It's not just your words that you are going to have to use in order to appeal to all of your audience's senses. Rather, your ability to add gestures and props to your speech is going to be what it will take to capture their attention.

Spices in your next speech are going to do you no good if you have just dumped them into your speech all in the same place. Just imagine how a meal would taste if you got a mouth full of some spice all at once! Instead, take the time to add some spice to your speech throughout the speech. Don't rush it – **spread it out**.

Finally, **don't over spice your speech**. You're going to look rather silly if your audience can only taste the spice in your next speech and they miss the main point of what you were trying to get across to them. Use your speech spice sparingly and only add it where it is going to help to make your message memorable.

What All Of This Means For You

A bland speech is very much like a bland meal – instantly forgettable. As speakers we need to find ways to **add some "spice"** to our next speech in order to make it both tasty while we are delivering it and memorable by our audience for how good it was.

In order to make this happen, we need to take the time to **add the right things to our speech**. This means finding ways to appeal to all of our audience's senses so that we'll be able to form a lasting memory. We can do this by ensuring that our speech is descriptive and dynamic, that we are organized, and that we are careful to not over do the spices.

Moderation is the key to making a good meal and the same thing can be said when we are creating a speech. We need to do what a good cook does and **be constantly sampling our own speech** to make sure that it's not too bland and not too spicy. Get your speech spices right and your audience is sure to want to come back for more.

Chapter 9

Public Speakers Know That They Have To Color Their Presentations

Chapter 9: Public Speakers Know That They Have To Color Their Presentations

Congratulations, you've been asked to give a speech. Were you thinking about using some PowerPoint or Keynote slides with that presentation?

One quick question about those slides that you're going to be making – do you know how to make the data that you are going to be presenting memorable **or is it just going to be forgettable?**

The Power Of Color

When we are putting together our slide decks, what do we spend our time thinking about? More often than not it's about **how many slides we are going to be creating** and what cool clip art we can use (or even worse: what cool animation we can add).

It turns out that we might be overlooking one of the most important factors that can cause our audiences to remember what we show them. **What we've been skipping is color**. Oh, I don't mean that we don't use color in our slides – no B&W decks here. However, if you are like most speakers then what color something is can almost be an afterthought.

This means that we've been missing the boat. Often times what we have is a lot of data that we want our audience to see. However, the real meaning of that data is hidden and it's up to us to **tease it out** and make sure that our audience understands it. This is where color can help us out.

If you've ever watched one of those fancy fashion shows, then you understand **just how powerful color can be in conveying information**. Your audience is going to be drawing conclusions from the images that you present to them in your slides. The colors that you use to do this are going to play a critical role in how effective this all is.

The color experts have studied how we process colors and they've learned a few things. One of the most important things is that **when we can name a color**, then we are better able to both understand and communicate the information that it contains. That's why using "ice" blue when you are talking about climate change will boost your audience's understanding of your message.

Problems That Using Color Can Cause

As powerful as spending extra time picking the correct colors to use in your next presentation can be, **it does come with its own set of challenges**. What we need to keep in mind as presenters is that the way that our deck of slides looks to us may not be the way that it looks to our audience.

We need to be aware that in our audiences, there will probably be people who have partial sight and color deficiencies. Since we want our message to connect with them just as much as with everyone else, we need to **adjust how we use colors** in order to meet their special needs.

This means that we need to **not use colors of similar lightness next to each other**. Simple steps like this will help the 285 million people world-wide who are visually impaired and the 246 million people who have low vision.

What All Of This Means For You

As public speakers we are always looking for ways to **improve our ability to connect with our audiences**. It turns out that we may have been overlooking a simple way to improve how we do this by using colors more effectively.

The experts who study such things tell us that our audience will always be using our images **to reach conclusions** and by using colors we can help steer them towards the conclusions that we want them to reach. We do need to be careful in how we use our colors and keep in mind that some of the members of our audience may have partial sight or color deficiencies issues.

Moving the selection of what colors we are going to use in our next presentation from being an afterthought **to being one of our first decisions** is easy enough to do. Now all we need to do is to make sure that the colors that we select help us to do a better job of telling our audience the story that we want them to hear.

Chapter 10

Create PowerPoint Slides, Go To Jail

Chapter 10: Create PowerPoint Slides, Go To Jail

Argh! There never seems to be enough time to pull that next presentation together. Somehow we always seem to find ourselves rushing around way too late in the process throwing our PowerPoint or Keynote decks together.

We all know that images are important and so it's all too easy to have Mr. Google go out and find that one perfect image or quote that so nicely sums up what you are trying to say. However, by doing this **have you just broken the law?**

All About That Copyright Thing

I'm sure that we've all heard about copyrights before, but do any of us really understand what they are? A copyright comes into existence when a creator creates a work. The copyright is **a bundle of rights** that relate to that work. The work could be a technical paper, a book, a movie, a photograph, etc.

The copyright owner has **5 different rights** that are all related to the work that they have created. They can reproduce the work in copies. They can distribute the copies of their work that they've made. They can display their work. They can perform their work (this is especially important for audio works). Finally, they can also create derivative works that are based on their original work.

What happens **if you "borrow" too much of someone's work?** Violating copyright law will depend on what country you are working in, but generally breaking a copyright law can carry both a civil and perhaps even criminal penalties. As speakers we can quote from other people's works, but we need to be careful to not quote too much and to make sure that we attribute the quote correctly.

How Can Speakers Prevent Themselves From Breaking The Law

As speakers, sometimes we just don't have the right way of saying something. If we find that someone else either said it better than we can or they created an image that perfectly captures what we're trying to communicate, then we'd really like to work their work into our speech. The question is **how best to do this without violating copyright laws?**

First off, you'll want to find out if the work that you want to use in your speech **is covered under a copyright**. The rules state that a copyright lasts for as long as the author is alive plus 70 years for any work that was not published before January 1st, 1978. Other rules apply to works that were created before then.

In order to use a work that is covered by a copyright, the simplest thing to do is to **ask the author for their permission for you to use their work**. The person who holds the copyright may be the author, their employer, or the estate of the author. Taking the time to get this permission can save you a world of grief later on.

What Does This Mean For You?

As speakers we generally have a single focus: presenting the best speech possible for our audience. In our effort to do this, **we can all too easily "borrow" material** that really belongs to another author be it images or words. If we step too far over the line, then we've just broken the laws that surround copyrights.

A copyright is a bundle of rights that the person who originally created a work reserves. This includes the right to reuse their work. **If you don't have permission from them to use their work, then you can't.**

As speakers we need to take the time to do our homework and determine if the work that we are using is protected by a copyright. If it is, then we need to seek out permission from the creator to use it.

Your audience has shown up to hear what you have to say, not to hear you share what somebody else said. No matter how good of a job that they did, **you need to be very careful to not use too much of their work**.

Yes, you can reference it, but no you can't copy it. Take the time to make sure that you remain on the right side of the copyright fence and you'll be safe every time you give a speech.

Chapter 11

6 Tips For Making PowerPoint Work With Your Next Speech, Not Against It

Chapter 11: 6 Tips For Making PowerPoint Work With Your Next Speech, Not Against It

How many times have you been asked to give a speech and the way that you got ready for it was to sit down and create a whole bunch of PowerPoint (or Keynote) slides? Yep, I've done the same thing.

Hopefully we all know that a speech is really so much more than just a bunch of slides. However, the slides that we use **can help to make our speech that much more effective**. How can we create slides that will help, not hinder, our next speech?

6 Tips For Making Better Slides

It is possible to give a speech without using any slides. Given the importance of public speaking, this is the right way to start to think about your next speech: how would I do it without any slides? Once you can picture what this would look like and you've got your speech built, then **it's time to come back and start to add slides**.

The purpose of using slides in your next speech needs to be to make a great speech even better. Each slide that you show to your audience needs to **enhance the point that you are trying to make in your speech** at that time. You don't want to confuse your audience and you don't want to take away from what you are trying to communicate.

Here are **6 tips to keep in mind** when you are deciding how you want the slides that will support your speech to look:

1. **Keep It Simple:** The PowerPoint tool comes with a lot of options that can be used to add cheesy effects to any slide. Avoid the temptation to dress up your slides using all of the tools at your disposal and instead keep your

focus on simple basic designs. Your audience will thank you for this.

2. **Make Your Text Easy To Read:** Yes, I know that you have a virtually unlimited number of fonts that are available for you to use, but don't use them! Instead, choose to use sans serf fonts (the simple looking ones without the fancy details). The best fonts for use with a PowerPoint slide include Arial, Helvetica, or Calibri. These fonts tend to be the easiest to read on screens.

3. **Use Decorative Fonts Sparingly:** I know that I can't talk you out of not using all of those fonts that you have at your fingertips, so let's see if I can get you to use them only occasionally. Try to use decorative fonts only for slide headers, and then only if they're easy to read. Generally speaking, decorative fonts are hard to read and should only be used for large headlines at the top of the page. I recommend that you stick to a classy serif font like Georgia or Baskerville.

4. **Love That Contrast:** The worst thing that you can do is to put dark text on a dark background or light text on a light background. Instead, put dark text on a light background. It turns out that this is the easiest to read. If you have to use a dark background (if your company uses a standard template with a dark background) make sure your text is quite light (white, cream, light grey or pastels) and maybe increase the font size.

5. **Stay Out Of The Middle Of The Road:** When you are adding text to a slide, you are going to want to align your text to the left or to the right. Centered text is harder to read and looks amateurish. Align your text with a right-hand or left-hand baseline – it will look better and be easier to follow.

6. **Reduce, Reduce, Reduce:** Always make sure that you avoid clutter. Keep the amount of material that you have on a slide to a minimum: a headline, a few bullet points, maybe an image – anything more than that and you risk losing your audience as they sort it all out.

What All Of This Means For You

As speakers, our goal is **to be able to connect with our audience**. It takes a lot of effort to create and deliver a speech. We want to maximize the impact that our speech is going to have. PowerPoint slides can help to make our speech do a better job of getting our point across to our audience and enhance the benefits of public speaking.

However, if we aren't careful, our PowerPoint slides can both distract and confuse our audience. That's why we need to take the time to create slides that will **work with our speech**, not against it. We've discussed 6 different tips that will help us to make slides that will complement our next speech.

Making high quality slides that act as an effective part of your next speech does not require a degree in art. Rather, what is required is an understanding of what it is going to take in order to **connect with your audience**. Use these tips and watch your next set of PowerPoint slides help your speech to become even more effective.

Chapter 12

How To Use PowerPoint To Create Intrigue In Your Next Presentation

Chapter 12: How To Use PowerPoint To Create Intrigue In Your Next Presentation

One of the challenges of any presentation is that we want to be able to both **capture and hold our audience's attention** while we are speaking. If your speech is 30 minutes, 60 minutes, or even longer this can be a real challenge. The good news is that your PowerPoint (or Keynote) slides can help you if you know how to add a bit of intrigue to your presentation...

The Problem – Solution Structure

Just about every speech that we give is delivered for a reason. No matter if you are trying to convey some information, convince your audience to see things your way, or sell an idea, **the ability to structure your speech as a "pitch" is a critical speaker skill** and is part of the importance of public speaking.

I know that many of us don't consider ourselves to be a "sales person"; however, you will still often find yourself in a situation where you want to **win your audience over to your way of thinking**. The big question is how to go about doing this.

One way to go about doing this is to create some intrigue by using **the problem-solution structure**. This is a way of crafting your speech in order to lead your audience to the conclusion that you want them to reach. Here is the process for structuring a speech in this fashion:

- Did you know? (a fact or statistic. A problem that costs time or money)
- Did you know? (2nd fact or problem)
- Did you know? (3rd fact or problem)
- What if? Imagine. (here you present the ideal solution)
- You don't have to imagine it; we've created it!

How To Use PowerPoint To Create Intrigue

Once you've got the problem-solution structure down, your next task is to find a way to **"hook" your audience** from the start. Your PowerPoint slides can help you to do this.

One of the biggest problems that we all have is that all too often when we are creating the slides that we are going to use in our presentation, **we start at the end**. We think about what the message that we want to communicate to our audience is and then we create a slide that shows exactly what we are trying to say. It turns out that this is the wrong thing to do.

Instead, we need to create PowerPoint slides that will create some intrigue for our audience. What this means for you is that you are not going to want to put all of your information onto a single slide – leave some or most of what you want to communicate **off of your slide**.

The experts have a name for this technique. They call it **"visual cognitive dissonance"**. What it means is that your audience will see the slide that you are showing them, but they will want to know more. What is the Y-axis showing them? What do the boxes mean? Since the slide isn't answering their question, their attention turns to you in order to get the answers that they are seeking.

Another term for what is going on here is **"anticipation"**. You can use a series of PowerPoint slides that gradually reveal more and more information to your audience. As each slide is revealed, your audience will want to know more. You'll have their attention from your first word to your last!

What All Of This Means For You

Every presenter wants to capture and hold his or her audience's attention for the length of their entire speech. Needless to say in today's iPhone, iPad, and short attention span world this can be very hard to do. That's why we need to **add some intrigue to our next speech**.

It turns out that you can build a presentation that grabs your audience's attention from the start. What you need to do is to use the problem – solution structure to grab their interest. Then use your PowerPoint slides to present some, but not all of your information. Your audience will be **eager to listen to you** in order to find the answers to their questions.

The human mind is a wonderful thing. It's always striving to get answers to questions. If as a presenter you offer your audience a series of **unanswered questions**, then you'll be able to keep their attention as long as they believe that you'll eventually be answering the questions that you've asked. Add some intrigue to your next presentation and watch what happens…!

It's from the forge of failure that the steel of success is formed.

Hard Work Does Not Guarantee Success, But Success Does Not Happen Without Hard Work.

- Dr. Jim Anderson

Create Speeches That Motivate Your Audiences And Get Your Message Heard!

Dr. Jim Anderson is available to provide training and coaching on the topics that are the most important to people who have to speak in public: how can I create a speech that people want to hear and how can I deliver in a way that will allow me to connect with my audience and get my point across to them?

Dr. Anderson believes that in order to both learn and remember what he says, speakers need to laugh. Each one of his speeches is full of fun and humor so that what he says "sticks" with everyone.

Dr. Anderson's Public Speaking Training Includes:

1. How to plan your next speech: pick your purpose and understand your audience.
2. What's the best way to get PowerPoint and Keynote to work with you, not against you?
3. What do you need to do when you are presenting in order to truly connect with your audience?

Dr. Jim Anderson presents over 100 speeches per year. To invite Dr. Anderson to speak at your event, contact him at: **Phone: 813-418-6970** or **Email:** jim@BlueElephantConsulting.com

Photo Credits:

Cover - By: Christophe Verdier
http://www.flickr.com/photos/cverdier/

Chapter 1 - By: David Feng
http://www.flickr.com/photos/fenng/

Chapter 2 - By: Boston Public Library
http://www.flickr.com/photos/boston_public_library/

Chapter 3 - By: Bossi
http://www.flickr.com/photos/thisisbossi/

Chapter 4 - By: snow
http://www.flickr.com/photos/venuste/

Chapter 5 - By: Gareth Saunders
http://www.flickr.com/photos/garethjmsaunders/

Chapter 6 - By: publik16
http://www.flickr.com/photos/publik16/

Chapter 7 - By: Morten Skogly
http://www.flickr.com/photos/mskogly/

Chapter 8 - By: david.moodley1
http://www.flickr.com/photos/52065931@N03/

Chapter 9 - By: Marshall Astor
http://www.flickr.com/photos/lifeontheedge/

Chapter 10 - By: Anirudh Koul
http://www.flickr.com/photos/anirudhkoul/

Chapter 11 - By: Jess Loughborough
http://www.flickr.com/photos/sunface13/

Chapter 12 - By: Joshua Gardner
http://www.flickr.com/photos/xdjio/

Other Books By The Author

Product Management

- Product Management Secrets: Techniques For Product Managers To Boost Product Sales And Increase Customer Satisfaction

- Product Development Lessons For Product Managers: How Product Managers Can Create Successful Products

- Customer Lessons For Product Managers: Techniques For Product Managers To Better Understand What Their Customers Really Want

- Product Failure Lessons For Product Managers: Examples Of Products That Have Failed For Product Managers To Learn From

- Communication Skills For Product Managers: The Communication Skills That Product Managers Need To Know How To Use In Order To Have A Successful Product

- How To Have A Successful Product Manager Career: The Things That You Need To Be Doing TODAY In Order To Have A Successful Product Manager Career

- Product Manager Product Success: How to keep your product on track and make it become a success

Public Speaking

- How To Give A Great Presentation: Presentation techniques that will transform a speech into a memorable event

- How To Rehearse In Order To Give The Perfect Speech: How to effectively rehearse your next speech to that your message be remembered forever!

- Secrets To Creating The Perfect Speech: How to create a speech that will make your message be remembered forever!

- Secrets To Organizing The Perfect Speech: How to organize the best speech of your life!

- Secrets To Planning The Perfect Speech: How to plan to give the best speech of your life

CIO Skills

- Critical CIO Management Skills: Decision Making Skills That Every CIO Needs To Have In Order To Be Able To Make The Right Choices

- How CIOs Can Make Innovation Happen: Tips And Techniques For CIOs To Use In Order To Make Innovation Happen In Their IT Department

- CIO Communication Skills Secrets: Tips And Techniques For CIOs To Use In Order To Become Better Communicators

- Managing Your CIO Career: Steps That CIOs Have To Take In Order To Have A Long And Successful Career

- CIO Business Skills: How CIOs can work effectively with the rest of the company!

IT Manager Skills

- Staffing Skills IT Managers Must Have: Tips And Techniques That IT Managers Can Use In Order To Correctly Staff Their Teams

- Secrets Of Effective Leadership For IT Managers: Tips And Techniques That IT Managers Can Use In Order To Develop Leadership Skills

- IT Manager Career Secrets: Tips And Techniques That IT Managers Can Use In Order To Have A Successful Career

- IT Manager Budgeting Skills: How IT Managers Can Request, Manage, Use, And Track Their Funding

<u>Negotiating</u>

- Learn The Skill Of Exploring In A Negotiation: How To Develop The Skill Of Exploring What Is Possible In A Negotiation In Order To Reach The Best Possible Deal

- Learn How To Argue In Your Next Negotiation: How To Develop The Skill Of Effective Arguing In A Negotiation In Order To Get The Best Possible Outcome

- How To Open Your Next Negotiation: How To Start A Negotiation In Order To Get The Best Possible Outcome

- Preparing For Your Next Negotiation: What You Need To Do BEFORE A Negotiation Starts In Order To Get The Best Possible Deal

Miscellaneous

- Power Distribution Unit (PDU) Secrets: What Everyone Who Works In A Data Center Needs To Know!

- Making The Jump: How To Land Your Dream Job When You Get Out Of College!

"How to use visual techniques to transform a speech into a memorable event"

> This book has been written with one goal in mind – to show you how you can use special tools when you deliver a speech. We'll cover how to use acting, PowerPoint, and word selection to create an unforgettable speech!
>
> **Let's Make Your Next Speech A Success!**

What You'll Find Inside:

- **TOOLS TO HELP VISUALIZE YOUR NEXT PRESENTATION**

- **MASTERING THE POWERPOINT BEAST IN 3 EASY STEPS**

- **SPEAKERS LEARN TO MAKE TASTY SPEECHES BY ADDING JUST THE RIGHT SPICES**

- **ACT UP OR SIT DOWN!**

Dr. Jim Anderson brings his 25 years of real-world experience to this book. He's delivered speeches at some of the world's largest firms as well as at many conferences. He's going to show you what you need to do in order to make your next speech a success!

www.ingramcontent.com/pod-product-compliance
Lightning Source LLC
Chambersburg PA
CBHW071803170526
45167CB00003B/1149